SHORT'S SUSSEX
PRINTS & SKETCHES BY SIR FRANK SHORT RA (1857-1945)

James Trollope

Published by SLATER
3 Edinburgh Road,
Seaford,
East Sussex
BN25 2PR
www.ericslater.co.uk

ISBN 978-1-9164798-0-7

Designed by Richard Mason of Bread and Butter Press
Printed and bound by Pureprint
October 2018

Cover image, *The Angry Cloud, Newhaven, 1930, mezzotint*

Acknowledgements

For allowing me to reproduce their images, I would like to thank Brighton Museum and Art Gallery (Jenny Lund), Worthing Museum and Art Gallery (Emma Walder), Rye Museum and Art Gallery (Jane Fenn, Julian Day) Towner, Eastbourne (Sara Cooper) and the Royal Academy (Jennifer Camilleri, Peter Sawbridge). I am also grateful to Libby Horner for the two photographs of Frank Short with Frank Brangwyn. She also made helpful comments on the draft and pointed me towards the letters of Frank Brangwyn. I would also like to thank Jane Allinson and her husband Derek on whose website (allinsongallery.com) I first saw Short's *The Shadowed Valley* thus becoming aware of the magnificence of Short's late mezzotints. Thanks to the family of John Bulloch Souter for permission to reproduce his portrait of Short. Thank you, as well, to Nic Small for his corrections. Any remaining mistakes are my own.

About the author

Having worked as a television reporter and newspaper columnist, James Trollope now writes mainly about art. He is the author of *Slater's Sussex* and *The Colour Woodcuts of Arthur Rigden Read,* both of which are available from **www.ericslater.co.uk**

SIR FRANK SHORT R·A
PRESIDENT·OF·THE·ROYAL·SOCIETY·OF·PAINTER–ETCHERS & ENGRAVERS TREASURER·OF·THE·ROYAL·ACADEMY.

Malcolm Osborne 1931.

CONTENTS

Portrait of Short, aged 74 by Malcolm Osborne, 1931, etching, fig 1

INTRODUCTION

In 1927 Sir Frank Short produced a stunning image of light scudding across the South Downs above Lewes. He was 70. Five years earlier, with retirement beckoning, he had bought a house nearby on the coast at Seaford. After a demanding career based in London, where he had established himself as the pre-eminent printmaker of his generation, the veteran artist found renewal in the landscape of Sussex.

Short's knowledge of printmaking was unsurpassed, influencing hundreds of artists from Whistler to Ravilious (1). He had run an etching class at the Royal College of Art for 33 years (2) and garnered a knighthood and several other honours in the process. (3). But the method he chose for his vision of the South Downs was very much his own. Almost single-handedly he championed the art of the original mezzotint - a technique which, unlike etching, involves working from black to white. The atmospheric results can look startlingly modern, resembling some of the best monochrome photography.

The Shadowed Valley, 1927 mezzotint, fig 2

Short's view of Oxteddle Bottom and Mount Caburn, which he called *The Shadowed Valley*, featured in an annual of the finest prints of that year (4). "The Shadowed Valley is a masterpiece

indeed," wrote the annual's editor Malcolm Salaman, "and I cannot recall in the whole range of his original work…that he has done anything quite so noble and stately. The curved lines…would seem to bring it arbitrarily within the category of 'modern art' but the structure of the land commands its own lines and curves and the moving clouds in the sky subtly rule its changing surface tones. So modern art truly happens when the artist has the genius to make it with beauty and truth."

Short made around 400 prints during his lifetime including about a hundred reproductive mezzotints, many after designs

Seaford Head, October 1924
pastel, fig 3

Towards Newhaven, October 1931, pastel, fig 4

by his hero JMW Turner (5), but after a professional life marked by duty, hard work and self-discipline he enjoyed an artistic release in 'retirement', not only a series of Sussex mezzotints but pastels, watercolours and etchings mostly inspired by the landscape within a few miles of his Seaford home. Like many ageing artists he felt compelled to achieve all he could in whatever time that was left to him.

From his window he had a direct view of the sea with the bay stretching westwards from Seaford Head to the cliffs at Newhaven. With pastels in hand, he made sketches from sunrise to sunset.

The freedom he found in old age was the climax of an association with Sussex, which ranged across 60 years. In his 20s he made prints of Rye, in his 30s of Bosham, in his 40s of Arundel and in his 50s of Winchelsea. However, many of his most memorable images were made in Seaford in his 60s, 70s and 80s.

Chapter One
SEAFORD

Although Short was born in the Midlands (6) he loved the sea. There are not many British towns further from the coast than his birthplace of Stourbridge in Worcestershire but he was drawn to the beaches, marshes and rivers of Sussex.

As a young man he had joined the Royal Navy Volunteer Reserve (7) with his great friend Frank Brangwyn and the two artists were reunited in Sussex in later life. Indeed, one of the reasons that Short chose Seaford may well have been its proximity to Brangwyn's house at Ditchling.

Seaford now has a population approaching 30,000 but in the 1920s fewer than 7,000 lived in the unpretentious town midway between Brighton and Eastbourne. Short's large semi-detached house, called Ingleside, was on Claremont Road overlooking the railway and a recreation ground called The Salts. The sea, just beyond, was less than a mile from his front door.

He and his wife Esther maintained their London home in Hammersmith (8) but after her death in 1925 Short spent more time on the coast with his daughter Dorothea keeping house and helping to mount his pictures (9). His other child Francis, a

MORNING DIP, SEAFORD.

Seaford between the wars, fig 5

captain in the West Kent Regiment, had died during the First World War (10).

Seaford was then best known for its mass of small private schools. At the beginning of each term Short would have seen and heard crowds of schoolchildren jostling on the station platform which had been made especially long for the purpose. Seaford was also home to a scattering of artists including three others who specialised in printmaking.

Eric Slater, who moved to the town in 1929, mastered a Japanese method of colour printing to make a series of woodcuts of Sussex (11).

Claremont Road, Seaford   Valentines Series

Short's white semi-detached house appears on this postcard of Claremont Road, Seaford, fig 6

DN Morgan (12), the son of the town's doctor William Pringle Morgan (the first to diagnose dyslexia), favoured the linocut technique for his images of Sussex. Norman Hirst (13), who spent a decade in the town from 1922, was the closest to Short in terms of technique, for he too was one of the very few artists of the period to specialise in mezzotint - the medium in which Short excelled.

Seaford Head Evening, 1927
watercolour, fig 7

Chapter Two
MEZZOTINTS

Short was in love with the velvety black tones of the mezzotint. For him they were a perfect match with the wet and windy night-time weather which is all too familiar to anyone who has ever lived in Seaford.

In a lecture to the print collectors' club in 1924 he told his audience that the mezzotint (half tone) was sometimes known in Germany as 'schwarzkunst' (the black art) and 'l'insicione a fumo' (engraving in smoke) in Italy. "In richness and power of tone and in perfection of gradation it has no rival." (14).

Put simply, the metal printing plate is roughened so as to hold ink. This is done with a tool called a rocker - a curved serrated chisel that is rocked back and forth across the plate to produce a rough ground of tiny ridges called burr. Short reckoned it took about a day to roughen a square foot, which, once the ink is added resembles 'a plate of metal velvet'. The artist then makes his design by scraping away some of the burr for lighter areas or by removing it altogether with a burnishing tool for pure light. Since it is the burr, which holds the ink, it is by scraping and burnishing that a range of tones can be achieved. His Seaford mezzotints show him to be an absolute master of the method.

Headlights over the Hill, 1927 mezzotint, fig 8

16

There's a touch of black and white movie in *Headlights over the Hill* (fig 8) but this arresting image is not Steven Spielberg in extra-terrestrial mood but Frank Short capturing the headlights of a car as it breasts a bump in the three-mile stretch of road leading from Seaford Head to Newhaven.

In *The Angry Cloud* (fig 9), a mile or two down the coast from Seaford Head, Short looks across at a dramatic sky towards the lighthouse at Newhaven. The sea crashes against a breakwater - a reminder that in Short's time the sea road, which runs alongside the beach, was often flooded. In the 1980s (15) the beach was bolstered with imported pebbles which the waves still occasionally scatter across the road.

Another print which wouldn't have pleased the local tourist board is *Wet Evening at Seaford* (fig 10). Short takes a few paces back from the previous view revealing the 'lost' village of Tide Mills and Newhaven lighthouse from the other side of the sea road. The beach buildings have long since disappeared but today's residents will be familiar with the weather, which the mezzotint technique evokes so tellingly.

The Angry Cloud, 1930, mezzotint, fig 9

Wet Evening, Seaford, 1933
mezzotint, fig 10

Before a bypass was opened in the 1960s, vehicles going to and from Newhaven, like this Southdown bus, had no alternative but to take the sea road. In stormy weather the road was sometimes impassable and the defensive wall was often breached as in the bottom left of picture. As it passes the old coastguard cottages at dusk, the bus heads towards the Buckle Inn (16) with the lights of Newhaven in the distance. The cottages and the inn are no more but memories of the treacherous road endure.

Southdown bus approaching the Buckle Inn, 1936, mezzotint, fig 11

Chapter Three
SUSSEX IN COLOUR

While the velvety tones of mezzotint were perfect for portraying Sussex in sombre mood, Short often turned to watercolour, pastel and, less frequently, to oils (17) when he wanted to celebrate the beauty of his adopted county. He was addicted to sunsets and from his window he dashed off scores of sky and seascapes with a spontaneity that is not evident in much of his printed work, which often demanded days of planning and execution.

Seaford Sunset, c1930, pastel, fig 12

Haven Brow, 1932, pastel, fig 13

At first glance some of his pastels resemble joyful scribbles but they have a vigour and charm which repay repeated viewing. In his later years, many were in sight of his home or around Cuckmere Haven, about two miles away.

One of his first watercolours after moving to Seaford was the classic view of the beach at Cuckmere Haven (fig 15).

A few years later he produced a study of the River Cuckmere winding its way towards Alfriston (fig 14).

While his watercolours are generally less distinctive than his mezzotints, many have historical as well as artistic merit. For example, there are few existing illustrations of the village of Tide Mills (fig 16), which lay between Seaford and Newhaven. The eponymous flourmill, powered by the tide, employed about 100 workers throughout much of the 19th century until it was demolished in 1883. When Short painted his view in the 1920s the population had dwindled and by 1936 the village was condemned, although a few residents hung on until the outbreak of war.

Short's watercolour shows a group of substantial buildings where now little but rubble remains. By the mid-1920s many of Short's subjects were confined to a five-mile radius of Seaford. He made dozens of studies of Seaford Head at all times of day and in all types of weather.

Cuckmere Haven, 1922 watercolour, fig 14

The River Cuckmere, 1928, watercolour, fig 15

Tide Mills, c1925, watercolour, fig 16

Chapter Four
ETCHINGS & AQUATINTS

Short was a craftsman to his fingertips. He not only knew how to use his tools, he often made them himself. In his blue overalls (18) he relished the technical side of his art and was generous in passing on his knowledge to others. Having left school at 13 and qualified as an engineer he became a master printmaker, summing up his credo thus: "An artist must be a workman; and an artist afterwards, if it please God."

Hundreds of students benefitted from his etching classes. One of them, Martin Hardie (19) described his teacher as: "physically strong, with a powerful frame, a massive head and large benevolent eyes, he was a man of quiet manner and kindly impulse but of firm character and great strength of will."

A distinguished artist in his own right, Hardie went on to catalogue Short's 400 or so prints, more than half of which were original etchings. While mezzotints are about tone, etchings focus on line, as Short makes clear in his handbook *On the Making of Etchings* (fig 41) which ran to several editions. To summarise, in mezzotint the design is worked directly on to the plate whereas in etching (and aquatint) acid plays a key part. The plate, usually copper, is covered with a coating of wax called 'ground'. The artist

Frank Short, c1900, fig 18

draws on the ground with a needle, ploughing through it to reveal the metal beneath. The plate is then immersed in acid, which bites into the metal. The sunken lines are filled with ink and transferred to paper through a press.

As with most printing methods, the image on the plate is made in reverse so it prints the right way round. The artist can shade from light grey to black by a process called 'stopping out' which controls the exposure of different parts of the image to acid. Short sometimes drew with a heavier needle directly on to the plate without using acid in a technique halfway between etching and engraving called 'drypoint' (20).

Aquatint is a tonal process like mezzotint but one which involves acid like etching. Put simply, the plate is sprinkled with grains of acid resistant resin, which produce a watercolour effect seen in some of Short's most subtle images like *Morning Haze in Chichester Harbour* (fig 19).

Short often visited the harbour and the neighbouring inlet of Bosham where he made a series of etchings in 1887 including *Washing Day* (fig 20) which Frank Brangwyn much admired (21).

Short returned to the area several times, producing watercolours and aquatints as well as etchings. His talent for evoking wide open spaces with an economy of line fitted well with the flatter landscape characteristic of Bosham and Chichester harbour, to the west of the county, and Winchelsea and Rye to the east.

*Washing day, Bosham, 1887
etching, fig 20*

As Hardie noted: "He shows a special love for … low-lying landscape with far-stretching meadows or shelving shore, or sands and harbours where the tide has ebbed." (22)

*Winchelsea Marshes, 1910,
etching, fig 21*

Rye Terrace, 1888, etching, fig 23

While Short's original mezzotints are often dramatic and bold, his etchings tend to be modest, even reticent. Although he found his subjects both at home and abroad, Sussex was a lifelong theme. One of his first etchings was of Rye in 1884, when he was 27.

The Strand Gate, Winchelsea, 1912, etching, fig 24

He often returned to Rye and neighbouring Winchelsea.

Curiously, some of his later Seaford images are printed the 'wrong way round' suggesting he drew the image directly on to the plate rather than reversing it before printing as is normally the case (23).

Rather than presenting *The Sea Road into Seaford* and *Rough Weather at Blatchington* as Short produced them they are shown here the 'right way round' with Seaford Head in its customary place

*The Sea Road into Seaford, 1925,
etching, fig 25*

*Rough Weather at Blatchington
1925, etching, fig 26*

37

Chapter Five
THE TWO FRANKS

The close friendship between Frank Short and Frank Brangwyn began when they were naval reservists together in the 1880s and had neighbouring studios in Chelsea (24).

When they reconnected in the 1920s they both found themselves widowers living in Sussex. After Brangwyn's wife, Lucy, died in 1924 he lived full time in a rambling house called 'The Jointure' in the downland village of Ditchling where he had retreated during the First World War to escape Zeppelin raids over London. The couple had no children.

Short's wife, Esther, died the following year, after which he spent less time in London and more in Seaford with his daughter Dorothea. "His daughter is a wonderful woman who has devoted her life to him," wrote Brangwyn who had a faithful housekeeper called Lizzie Peacock (25) to look after him.

The two Franks had a mutual friend called Matthew Walker (26) who sometimes acted as a dealer for both artists. Letters between Brangwyn and Walker show that the three men met regularly in Sussex with Walker often called upon to chauffeur Short to Ditchling or Brangwyn to Seaford.

Short (from back) and Brangwyn (far right), naval reservists, fig 27

"It is most kind of you to have taken me to see Short. I enjoyed it and your company," writes Brangwyn in September 1933, adding, as he often did, news (invariably negative) about his health. "I am not feeling well. I still feel very giddy and unfit for work."

Brangwyn was then aged 66, ten years younger than Short. His impressive body of work was mostly on a larger scale than the older Frank, whom he often referred to as 'dear old' or 'poor old' Short. Internationally known for his murals (27) and oil paintings, Brangwyn also produced about 500 etchings.

Brangwyn (far left), Short (middle) and Walker at The Jointure, fig 28

While Short favoured small landscapes, Brangwyn tackled big themes including war, industry and religion. He was also drawn to exotic, foreign subjects, making very few pictures of Sussex, although he had trenchant views about preserving the beauty of his adopted county.

On a visit to The Jointure in 1926 *The Sussex County Magazine* (28) reported that: "His chief grievance is against the petrol stations which look 'so sordid and are a hideous blot upon the landscape.' It is the same with the bungalows which have been 'dumped on the London to Brighton road. Some of them are little better than chicken runs yet bungalows and petrol stations could be beautiful things.' He considers the authorities should take up this matter 'strenuously'. "

During the 1930s, as the likelihood of war increased, Brangwyn began to worry about the fate of his pictures as well as his own safety, although it was Short who was under greater threat in his more exposed coastal location. In 1940, a year after making his last recorded print, Short's stay in Seaford came to abrupt end when a bomb landed on a train close to Ingleside and the artist and his daughter were forced to move inland (29).

Brangwyn, meanwhile, was arranging for much of his and Short's work to be stored in the Cotswolds, away from the heaviest enemy bombardment. He found storage at a house in Chipping Camden belonging to the widow of the artist F. L. Griggs (30) who had died in 1938. In a letter to Walker in January 1941 Brangwyn writes:

"I got a nice long letter from Short's girl. He seems to have been ill poor chap. I wish I could see him and have a crack. I suggested that he should send some of his stuff to Chipping Camden but he seems not to care much about what happens to his possessions."

A few months later Short rallied and in another letter to Walker Brangwyn reports that: "Short is well off with his girl to look after him. All his stuff at Chipping Camden is all right so far."
In 1943 Dorothea and her father decided to move to their Hammersmith house against the advice of Brangwyn. "I think our friend Short is silly to go back to all the worry and bother of London but he will not be told so he must go his own way."

In February the following year Brangwyn tells Walker that he's heard from Short that they are getting raids in London almost every night, adding: "I have had bladder trouble. I fear an operation, my legs and feet are full of rheumatism, my eyes are not up to much and I have aches and pains everywhere."

Despite these troubles, Brangwyn came to the rescue of his old friend and Dorothea. When the pair were bombed out of their London home in the summer of 1944 he offered them sanctuary in

Frank Short at The Jointure, 1944 by
John Bulloch Souter
(Royal Academy of Arts), fig 29

his garden studio at The Jointure (31).

In the following months Short, now 87, became increasingly frail. Brangwyn wrote to Walker in October. "Every night when I visit Short for an hour we talk of you. How fine it would be if you could join us. It is sad to see our dear friend. He cannot talk or move but is bright and his brain is as clear as ever. So we talk and, in a measure, I hope he is happy."

Around this time the artist John Bulloch Souter (32) came to visit and painted a portrait of the invalid. Seated in an armchair, Short is engaged in a favourite pastime - examining prints: "…prints of your very own that you take out of your Solander case or portfolio; prints you hold tenderly in your hand, turn into various lights, and lift from the mount to enjoy the very feel of the paper: proofs that you have learned line by line, and yet in which you are always finding new meaning… when the work of the day is done, and the curtains are drawn, and these prints come out, is there ever a time when life seems better?" (33)

Short died on April 22nd, 1945 aged 87 - some six months after moving to Ditchling. Two days later Brangwyn wrote to Walker:

"No doubt you have seen in the papers that our dear old friend Short has passed away. In the last few weeks of his life he had a lot of pain caused by a clot. I saw him in the two or three days before he passed away, poor old dear. So far his girl bears up very well. It is a great blow to her as she was devoted to him. It was wonderful how she nursed him, like a mother with her child."

Seascape, Seaford, c1925
pastel, fig 30

Chapter Six
LEGACY

His former pupil and friend, Martin Hardie, described Short as "an engineer with the soul of an artist" (34). An artist, moreover, whose work, despite changing fashions, was in demand throughout his life. Even in those final months at The Jointure, London art dealers Conalghi (35) were busy preparing an exhibition of his prints.

He certainly made his mark on generations of artists as a teacher and was the first printmaker in the twentieth century to become a full member of the Royal Academy. He was President of The Royal Society of Painter-Etchers and Engravers and knighted 30 years before Brangwyn (36). His series of mezzotint reproductions of landscape studies by Turner may have been his greatest challenge but, for me, his original mezzotints are his outstanding legacy.

For all the understated charm of his original etchings, pastels and watercolours, these bold images with their velvety blacks can take the breath away. Many of the most memorable were produced in Seaford where he was free from teaching. With Dorothea's support he was able to follow his own artistic impulses; to look out of his window at the sea and the sky; to observe the sunsets, the moon and the shifting clouds; to capture his chosen stretch of Sussex in

Sunset, c1930, pastel, fig 31

all its moods whether in print, crayon or watercolour. As we have seen it took a world war to end this fertile, late-flowering period.

In the year after his death Brighton Museum and Art Gallery held a memorial exhibition featuring 145 of his works many of Sussex (37). In the catalogue, museum director Clifford Musgrave (38) praised his etchings and aquatints for their "genius in expressing the sense of infinity" and his original mezzotints "in which perhaps he found himself best able to convey his deepest poetical feelings."

Dorothea kept her father's flame alive and, on her death in 1973, bequeathed large collections of his work to Brighton, Worthing and Rye art galleries reflecting his deep attachment to his adopted county.

In recent years there has been a tendency to view Short as an establishment figure whose etchings are indistinguishable from many others of similar vintage. When the trend is for self-publicists it is easy to overlook the merits of a modest man who elevated his craft to an art which ripened in old age.

Newhaven, c1930, watercolour, fig 32

CAREER
TIMELINE

This book has been mainly concerned with Short after his retirement from the Royal College of Art in 1924. Here's a brief outline of his life and career before then.

1918 portrait of Sir Frank Short by Arthur Hacker (1858-1919), Royal Academy of Arts, fig 33

1857   Born Stourbridge.

1883   Leaves Stourbridge as a qualified civil engineer to study art in London joining an etching class at the Royal College of Art.

1885   Elected member of the Royal Society of Painter-Etchers and Engravers (RE). Encouraged by Ruskin begins work on completing Turner's *Liber Studiorum* (fig 34).

1888   Writes his book *On the Making of Etchings*.

1889   Awarded a Gold medal at the Paris Salon. Marries Esther Rosamund Parker.

1890   Birth of daughter Dorothea.

1891   Runs the etching class at the RCA for the next 33 years.

1892   Son Francis is born. Short has studio in Chelsea near to Frank Brangwyn.

1900   Wins another Gold medal at Paris Salon.

1906   Elected associate member of the Royal Academy.

1910   Knighted after becoming President of the Royal Society of Painter-Etchers and Engravers.

1911   Publishes *Etchings and Engravings*. Elected full member of the Royal Academy.

1916   Death of son Captain Francis Short.

1919   Becomes Treasurer of the Royal Academy until 1932.

1921   Becomes President of the Print Collectors' Club.

1922   Acquires Ingleside in Seaford where he lives on and off until 1939.

1924   Retires from the RCA.

Crowhurst, Sussex, 1902, mezzotint
after Turner, fig 34

THE MEZZOTINT TECHNIQUE

Short made these two prints to demonstrate his mezzotint technique.

This shows the work of the rocker. The upper lighter section was prepared in the same way as the lower darker part but has been scraped clear of burr to show how the rocker's teeth dig into the copper. The nine lines indicate the direction of the rocking.

Fig 35

Fully rocked, this shows the deep velvety black obtained by leaving the burr untouched and also the lighter shading, which can be made by partially removing the burr with a scraper.

Fig 36

NOTES

1 Whistler called on Short to express his admiration for one of Short's Bosham etchings, *Sleeping Till the Flood* (fig 43). Although 23 years older than Short he often asked him for technical advice. Short's verdict on Ravilious: "A clever student, experimenting a great deal but not easy to teach." *Ravilious & Co* by Andy Friend published by Thames & Hudson 2017.

2 Short ran the engraving school at the RCA from 1891 to 1924.

3 In 1911 Short was elected a full member of the Royal Academy where he was treasurer from 1919 to 1932. He was president of the RE from 1910 to 1938. He won gold medals for engraving at the Paris International Exhibitions of 1889 and 1900 and in 1917 was elected a member of the Royal Institute of Painters in Watercolours.

4 The annual *Fine Prints of the Year*, ran from 1923 to 1938. Malcolm Salaman (1855-1940), a leading art critic of the period, was the founding editor.

5 Turner began classifying different styles of landscape in a series of studies called *Liber Studiorum,* which were transformed by others

into mezzotints, 70 of which were made before his death. Working from Turner's drawings, Short completed the task adding more than 40 mezzotints. Martin Hardie, author of Short's catalogue raisonné described it as "the core of his life's work."

6   Short was born on June 19, 1857 at Wollaston, Stourbridge. His father, Job Till Short, was a bricklayer and engineer. His mother was Emma Millward.

7   In the 1880s the two artists did gunnery drill together on an old warship in West India Dock and made frequent sketches of sailors and ships (note by Peter Nahum, The Leicester Galleries).

8   Short moved to 56 Brook Green, Hammersmith in 1901 and kept the property until his death in 1945, after which it was sold by his daughter.

9   In 1952 Dorothea sent a print, *Headlights over the Hill*, to a friend called Sylvia Hands hoping it "would remind you of a merry holiday we spent together in Seaford years ago…I have mounted it the way father liked and always had them done, very often by me."

10   Francis trained as a lawyer and saw active service in France. He died in 1916 from endocarditis at the family home in Brook Green.

11   For more on Eric Slater (1896-1963) see *Slater's Sussex* by James Trollope published by Towner, 2013.

12   Between the wars DN Morgan (1895-1986) exhibited twice at the Walker Galleries in London. A teacher and bookbinder in later years, he also produced a collection of pen and ink drawings called *A Sketchbook of Seaford*.

13   Norman Hirst (1862-1956) lived in Seaford from 1922 to 1934 and was one of the few other artists to produce original mezzotints between the wars including some of Sussex.

14   From the Mezzotint chapter in Short's book *Etchings and Engravings*.

15   In 1987, before October's hurricane, 3 million tons of shingle was added to the beach in one of the largest operations of its kind ever undertaken in the UK.

16 The Buckle Inn was a landmark for nearly 200 years before it was demolished in 1962.

17 Brighton Museum and Art Gallery has two oil paintings by Short, one of Newhaven, the other of the Cuckmere Valley. Both are over 3ft long and can be viewed on artuk.org

18 A 1918 portrait of Short (fig 33) by Sir Arthur Hacker (1858-1919) shows him in his working garb of stained, blue overalls.

19 Martin Hardie (1857-1952) was in awe of Short as a teacher, describing how a twitch of his moustache could indicate approval (upwards) or otherwise (downwards). His three-volume catalogue of Short's printed work was essential in preparing this book.

20 Short gives an admirably clear account of his different printmaking techniques (etchings, dry-point, line engraving, aquatint and mezzotint) in his book *Etchings and Engravings*.

21 In September 1935 Brangwyn writes to Walker asking: "Have you found that little Short etching of the backs of the fishermen's cottages at Bosham? I want to work on a sketch from it."

22   From a 1913 article by Hardie for the *Wolverhampton Express &*
     Star to coincide with a Frank Short exhibition at the
     Wolverhampton Art Gallery.

23   In his later years Short, perhaps for reasons of speed, often drew
     directly on to the plate resulting in several images, including one
     of Seaford's Martello tower, being printed the wrong way round.
     In the case of the Martello tower Hardie notes that he made a few
     counter proofs 'to bring the subject the right way round for
     Seaford people.'

24   The studios were in Manresa Road, Chelsea. Some of the artists
     working there formed the Chelsea Arts Club and the New English
     Art Club.

25   Lizzie Peacock, who had worked for Brangwyn since 1904, was
     with him when he died in 1956. She insisted that they remained in
     Ditchling during the war when Brangwyn thought of
     moving to the Cotswolds. "Lizzie will not leave what she calls her
     home," wrote Brangwyn to Walker in January 1941.

26   Matthew Biggar Walker (1873-1950) was from Dudley and worked

at various times as a tailor, draper and school teacher before establishing himself as an art dealer and collector. He helped organise a number of exhibitions in Wolverhampton and elsewhere, donating works by Brangwyn, Short and others to various museums. His correspondence with Brangwyn, consisting of 242 letters (mostly from Brangwyn), is held by the Birmingham Museum and Art Gallery.

27 His most famous murals can be seen at Brangwyn Hall, Guildhall, in Swansea. They were destined for the House of Lords but, to Brangwyn's dismay, were deemed unsuitable. Nearer to his old home at Ditchling the murals at Christ's Hospital near Horsham tell the story of the Christian Church in Britain.

28 *The Sussex County Magazine* founded by Arthur Beckett (1872-1943) ran from December 1926 until June 1956.

29 "The playful Hun was over the coast here and dropped a bomb on a train which was right in front of Frank Short's house," writes Brangwyn in a letter to Walker dated July 7, 1940.

30 FL Griggs (1876-1938), a distinguished etcher and friend of Short.

31 The studio became vacant after the death of Brangwyn's previous tenant, the etcher William Walcott (1874-1943).

32 John Bulloch Souter (1890-1972) was a Scottish artist and print-maker, who became a successful portrait painter after moving to London in the 1920s. Ivor Novello and Gladys Cooper were among his other subjects.

33 From the penultimate paragraph of Short's book *Etchings and Engravings* first published in 1911.

34 A quote from Hardie's 1913 article in the *Wolverhampton Express and Star*.

35 Brangwyn asks Walker in a letter dated Oct 23, 1944 to lend some prints by Short to the Colnaghi show.

36 Frank Short was knighted in 1911 and Brangwyn in 1941.

37 The exhibition at Brighton Museum and Art Gallery ran from January 12 to February 3, 1946.

38 Dr Clifford Musgrave (1904-1982) was Director of Brighton Art Gallery and Museums and the Royal Pavilion and the author of *Life in Brighton*. As an executor of Dorothea Short's will, he ensured her father's work was well represented in local galleries. Like Short he retired to Seaford.

Memorial Exhibition Catalogue, fig 37

LIST OF ORIGINAL
SUSSEX PRINTS

*Low Tide & the Evening Star and Rye's
Long Pier Deserted, 1888
etching, fig 38*

Etchings and Drypoints (36)

1884   *Rye*, 12.7 x 22.5cm
Old Houses at Rye (dry-point), 20.1 x 15cm
The Astrea, Rye, 12.7 x 8.2cm

1887   *Sleeping Till the Flood, Bosham*, 15.2 x 20.1cm (fig 43)
The Patience, Bosham, 16.5 x 19cm
Evening, Bosham, 15.2 x 20.2cm
Nutbourne Mill, Bosham, 15.2 x 20.1cm
Fisherman's Castle, Bosham, 15 x 20cm
Washing Day, Bosham, 15 x 20.1cm (fig 20)

1888   *The Building of the Golden Bee, Bosham*, 15 x 20.1cm
Rye Port, 18.4 x 26cm
Last Days of an Old Brig, Rye, 15 x 19.9cm
Rye Terrace, 15 x 20.1cm (fig 23)
Low Tide & the Evening Star and Rye's Long Pier Deserted,
18.4 x 26.1cm (fig 38)

1890 *A Dead Calm in Itchenor Channel*, 12.6 x 17.7cm

1905 *Collier Entering Littlehampton*, 24.7 x 32.2cm

1907 *Houghton Bridge*, 18.6 x 31cm
Water Meadows, Arundel, 15.3 x 20cm
On the Banks of the Arun, 19.8 x 30cm
A Lane in Arundel, 20.7 x 25.3cm
Stopham Bridge, 17.4 x 25cm

1909 *In Arundel Park*, 19.6 x 29cm

1910 *Winchelsea Marshes*, 11.1 x 26.4cm (fig 21)
Strand Gate, Winchelsea, 18.3 x 31.5cm (fig 24)

1923 *Hobb's Hawth, Near Seaford*, 18.1 x 30.5cm

1925 *The Sea Road into Seaford*, 16 x 23.1cm (fig 25)
Rough Weather at Blatchington, Seaford, 14 x 22.1cm (fig 26)

1931   *Exceat, Cuckmere Valley,* 8.6 x 13.6cm
Seaford, 11.2 x 12.3cm
Seaford Head No 1, 25 x 35.1cm
Seaford Head No 2, 10.1 x 10.1cm

1932   *Haven Brow, Cuckmere Haven* (dry-point) 25.7 x 38.6cm

1936   *Chalk Cliffs at Cuckmere Haven, The Seventh Sister,* 30.1 x 22.6cm
(fig 42)

1938   *The Martello Tower, Seaford,* 17.5 x 25.2cm
The Old Rocket House, Seaford, 15.2 x 19.5cm

1939   *Hawk's Brow and Seaford Head* (dry-point), 13.1 x 32.8cm

Aquatints (7)

A Silver Tide, Bosham, 1912
aquatint, fig 39

1884 *Jeake's House, Rye,* 12.5 x 18cm

1887 *In Bosham Harbour,* 17.8 x 25cm

1888 *Rye Pier, Evening,* 12.2 x 21.6cm

1889 *Bosham,* 17.9 x 25cm
The Curfew, Rye, 15 x 20cm (fig 22)

1912 *A Silver Tide, Bosham,* 15.2 x 23.1cm (fig 39)

1922 *Morning Haze in Chichester Harbour,* 23.9 x 35cm (fig 19)

Mezzotints (8)

Exceat Farm, Seaford, and Hindover
1932, mezzotint, fig 40

1892 *Rye*, 10.2 x 15cm

1927 *Headlights over the Hill, Seaford*, 15 x 2.01cm (fig 8)
The Shadowed Valley, Near Lewes, 36.5 x 49.2cm (fig 2)

1930 *The Angry Cloud, Newhaven*, 150 x 22.6cm (fig 9)

1932 *Exceat Farm and Hindover, Cuckmere*, 28 x 40.5cm (fig 40)

1933 *Wet Evening, Seaford*, 17.5 x 25.1cm (fig 10)

1936 *The Harvest Moon Over Seaford Head*, 15.3 x 20.3cm

The Southdown Bus Approaching the Buckle Inn, 22.4 x 30cm (fig 11)

BIBLIOGRAPHY

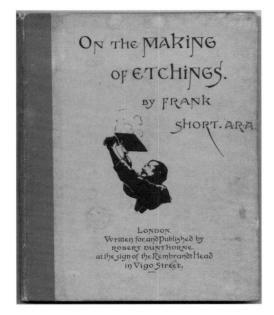

Fig 41

On the Making of Etchings, 1888, by Frank Short published by Robert Dunthorne.

Etchings and Engravings, 1911, by Frank Short published by the Royal Society of Painter-Etchers and Engravers.

Express and Star, 1913, article by Martin Hardie about Sir Frank Short exhibition at Wolverhampton Art Gallery.

British Mezzotints by Sir Frank Short, 1924, published by the Print Collectors' Club.

The Studio Magazine, Vol 88, Number 379, 1924, 'Sir Frank Short's Retirement from the Royal College of Art' by Malcolm Salaman.

Modern Masters of Etching Sir Frank Short by Malcolm Salaman, 1925, published by *The Studio.*

The Sussex County Magazine, 'Mr Brangwyn talks about Sussex' Vol 1, Nos 1 Dec 1926 published by T.R. Beckett Ltd.

Fine Prints of the Year 1927, edited by Malcolm Salaman, published by Halton and Truscott Smith.

Letters between Frank Brangwyn and Matthew Walker, Birmingham Museum and Art Gallery.

The Etched and Engraved Work of Sir Frank Short, Volume 1, The Liber Studiorum Mezzotints, Catalogue and Introduction by Martin Hardie, 1938, published by the Print Collectors' Club.

The Etched and Engraved Work of Sir Frank Short, Volume 2, The Mezzotints and Aquatints, Catalogue and Introduction by Martin Hardie, 1939, published by the Print Collectors' Club.

The Etched and Engraved Work of Sir Frank Short, Volume 3, Etchings, Dry-points, Lithographs, Catalogue and Introduction by Martin Hardie, 1940, published by the Print Collectors' Club.

A Memorial Exhibition of the Work of the Late Frank Short, 1946, Catalogue Introduction by Clifford Musgrave, published by Brighton Art Gallery.

British Printmakers 1855-1955, Garton & Co in association with Scolar Press.

No Day Without a Line, The History of the Royal Society of Painter-Printmakers 1880-1999 by Martin Hopkinson, published by Ashmolean Museum.

Bygone Seaford by John Odam, republished by Seaford Museum and Heritage Society, 2009

Seaford Through Time by Kevin Gordon, 2010, Amberley Publishing.

Chalk Cliffs at Cuckmere Haven
The Seventh Sister, 1936
etching, fig 42

Image Credits

Malcolm Osborne, Portrait of Short, 1931, etching, courtesy of Bonhams, copyright artist's estate

Frank Short, Seaford Head, 1924, pastel, Brighton Museum and Art Gallery (BMAG)

Frank Short, Towards Newhaven, c1925, pastel, Worthing Museum and Art Gallery (WMAG)

Frank Short, Wet Evening at Seaford, 1933, mezzotint, WMAG

Frank Short, Southdown Bus approaching the Buckle Inn, 1936, mezzotint, BMAG

Frank Short, Seaford, c1927, pastel, WMAG

Frank Short, Haven Brow, 1932, pastel, BMAG

Frank Short, Cuckmere Haven, 1922, watercolour, BMAG

Frank Short, The River Cuckmere, 1928, watercolour, BMAG

Frank Short, Tide Mills, c1927, watercolour, BMAG

Frank Short, Seaford Head, c1930, watercolour, BMAG

Frank Short, Rye terrace, 1888, etching, Rye Museum and Art Gallery (RMAG)

Frank Short and Frank Brangwyn naval photo, c1880, courtesy of Libby Horner

Brangwyn, Short and Walker, photo, c1925, courtesy of Libby Horner

John Bulloch Souter, Frank Short Portrait, 1944, oil on board, copyright artist's estate, photograph courtesy of the Royal Academy of Arts

Frank Short, Seaford Seascape, c1925, watercolour, WMAG

Frank Short, Sunset, c1930, pastel, WMAG

Frank Short, Newhaven, c1930, watercolour, WMAG

Arthur Hacker, Frank Short Portrait, 1918, oil on Canvas, photograph courtesy of the Royal Academy

Frank Short, Memorial Exhibition Catalogue, 1946, BMAG

Frank Short, Exceat Farm and Hindover, 1932, mezzotint, Towner, Eastbourne

Frank Short, Chalk Cliffs of Cuckmere Haven, The Seventh Sister, 1936, etching, RAMG

Unlisted images are from private collections

Sleeping Till the Flood, Bosham
1887, etching, fig 43

NB The author and publisher gratefully acknowledge the permission granted to reproduce material in this book. All reasonable efforts have been made to trace copyright holders and obtain permission for images used. The publisher apologises for any errors or omissions in this list, and would be grateful to be notified of any corrections that should be incorporated in future reprints or editions of this book